From Egg to Adult
The Life Cycle of Reptiles

Heinemann
LIBRARY

Mike Unwin

H **www.heinemann.co.uk/library**

Visit our website to find out more information about **Heinemann Library** books.

To order:

☎ Phone 44 (0) 1865 888066

🖹 Send a fax to 44 (0) 1865 314091

💻 Visit the Heinemann Bookshop at www.heinemann.co.uk/library to browse our catalogue and order online.

First published in Great Britain by Heinemann Library, Halley Court, Jordan Hill, Oxford OX2 8EJ, part of Harcourt Education Ltd.
Heinemann is a registered trademark of Harcourt Education Ltd.

© Harcourt Education Ltd 2003
First published in paperback in 2004
The moral right of the proprietor has been asserted.

Editorial: Nicole Irving and Georga Godwin
Design: Jo Hinton-Malivoire and AMR
Illustrations: David Woodroffe
Picture Research: Maria Joannou and Lizz Eddison
Production: Séverine Ribierre

Originated by Dot Gradations Ltd
Printed and bound in China

ISBN 0 431 16861 X (hardback)
07 06 05 04 03
10 9 8 7 6 5 4 3 2 1

ISBN 0 431 16868 7 (paperback)
08 07 06 05 04
10 9 8 7 6 5 4 3 2 1

British Library Cataloguing in Publication Data
Unwin, Mike
From egg to adult: The life cycle of reptiles
571.8'179
A full catalogue record for this book is available from the British Library.

Acknowledgements
The Publishers would like to thank the following for permission to reproduce photographs: Ardea/Adrian Warren p. **21**; Ardea/Frank Woerle p. **19**; Australia Zoo p. **25**; Bruce Coleman Collection/Fred Bruemmer p. **22**; Bruce Coleman/Gerald S. Cubitt p. **4**; Corbis p. **18**; FLPA/Albert Visage p. **29**; FLPA p. **23**; FLPA/E. & D. Hosking p. **7** (bottom); FPLA/K. Aitken/Panda p. **17** (bottom); NHPA pp. **16** (top), **16** (bottom), **24**; NHPA/Anthony Bannister pp. **11**, **13**; NHPA/Nigel J. Dennis p. **10**; NHPA/Stephen Dalton pp. **15**, **17** (top); NHPA/Daniel Heuclin p. **26** (top); NHPA/Karl Switak p. **5**; Oxford Scientific Films pp. **7** (top), **9**, **20**, **26**; Oxford Scientific Films/Breck P. Kent p. **12**; Oxford Scientific Films/Tom Ulrich p. **14**; Oxford Scientific Films/Mark Deeble p. **8**.

Cover photograph of the hatching turtle, reproduced with permission of Oxford Scientific Films.

The lizard at the top of each page is a water dragon.

The Publishers would like to thank Colin Fountain for his assistance in the preparation of this book.

Every effort has been made to contact copyright holders of any material reproduced in this book. Any omissions will be rectified in subsequent printings if notice is given to the Publishers.

Contents

Look but don't touch: many reptiles are very delicate and some can also be dangerous. If you see one in the wild, do not approach too close. Look at it but do not touch it!

Any words appearing in bold, **like this**, are explained in the Glossary.

What is a reptile?

Reptiles are **vertebrates**. Their bodies are supported by **endoskeletons**, they breathe air through lungs and their skin is dry, waterproof and covered in scales – very different from the cold, slimy body of an amphibian. There are over 6500 **species** of reptile in the world, including snakes, lizards, turtles, tortoises and crocodiles.

Living dinosaur

Dinosaurs were reptiles that lived on Earth long before people. Today, the tuatara is a living relative of the dinosaurs. This lizard-like reptile has hardly changed in 130 million years, though all its relatives have long since become **extinct**.

Warming up

Reptiles are sometimes called 'cold-blooded', but their blood is not always cold. In fact, they are ectothermic. This means their body temperature changes according to the temperature outside. Reptiles use sunshine to warm up their bodies and give themselves energy. This is why they are more common in warmer parts of the world.

The tuatara lives in rabbit burrows on small islands off the coast of New Zealand.

How are reptiles born?

Most reptiles lay eggs. Tortoise and crocodile eggs have hard shells, just like bird eggs. Snake, lizard and sea turtle eggs have soft, leathery shells. Some reptiles, such as geckos, lay only one or two eggs. Others, such as turtles or crocodiles, may lay over 100. Reptile eggs are on the menu for many animals, including storks, raccoons and mongooses. Reptiles with the most **predators** lay the most eggs. This gives more of their babies a chance to survive.

Life in the shell

Inside an egg, the baby reptile, or **embryo**, gets its food from the yolk. A liquid, called **amniotic fluid**, protects the embryo and yolk. Tiny holes in the eggshell, called pores, let in enough **oxygen** for the baby to breathe.

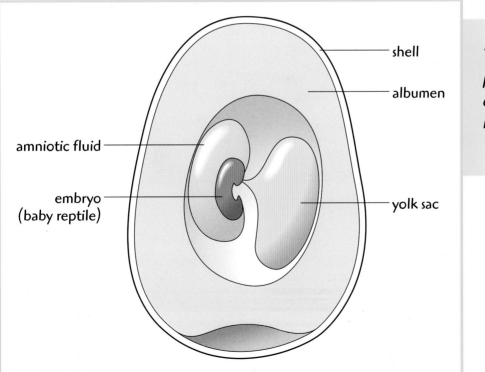

shell

albumen

amniotic fluid

embryo
(baby reptile)

yolk sac

The different parts inside a growing reptile egg.

Keeping eggs warm

Reptile eggs must be kept at just the right temperature for the babies inside to grow. This is called **incubation**. Most reptiles choose a warm, moist place to lay their eggs, such as under a log, in a compost heap, or buried in the sand. The temperature inside an egg determines whether the baby grows into a male or female. In crocodiles, a high temperature of 31°–34°C produces male babies, while a lower temperature of 26°–30°C produces females. With turtles and tortoises it is the other way round.

Most female reptiles leave their eggs to incubate and **hatch** on their own. Some, though, such as crocodiles and pythons, stay with their eggs. The parents keep the eggs warm and protect them from predators until they hatch.

A female green tree python coils tightly around her eggs to help keep them warm.

Breaking free

To help it get out, each baby reptile has a special sharp egg-tooth, which it uses to slice a hole in the shell. It then wriggles and pushes its way outside. Baby crocodiles and tortoises have an egg-tooth on the end of the nose; snakes and lizards have theirs sticking out from the upper lip. Egg-teeth drop off a few weeks after the babies hatch.

This baby terrapin has broken the shell with its egg-tooth.

Live young

Instead of laying eggs, some snakes and lizards that live in cooler parts of the world give birth to live babies. This means the embryo can develop inside the warm body of the mother, where it receives all the **nourishment** it needs to grow bigger.

The adder lives in cooler climates than most snakes. It gives birth to about twenty live young. They stay with their mother for a few days before heading off to find food.

Ready to go

Unlike many baby mammals and birds, baby reptiles can see, move about and feed as soon as they are born. They look just like miniature adult reptiles, but with brighter, shinier colours. Some babies are born with special markings, which disappear when they get bigger and older. These colours help to protect them.

A baby crocodile weighs only 250 grams when it hatches, but its mother may weigh 500 kilograms – over 2000 times heavier. This young crocodile is lying on its mother's foot!

Most small reptiles have large babies. A newly hatched baby gecko is about 5 cm long – one-third the length of its mother. Big reptiles have smaller babies. Baby green iguanas have markings on their closed eyelids that look just like open eyes. This means that predators think they are awake, even when they are asleep, so the predators leave them alone.

Who looks after baby reptiles?

Most baby reptiles never see their mothers – unlike baby mammals, whose mothers stay with them while they grow up. Some baby snakes stay near their mother for a few days, but she soon leaves, and they have to start looking after themselves.

Scramble for the sea

A female sea turtle comes ashore to bury her eggs in the dry sand at the top of a beach. There they are hidden from **predators** and the waves will not wash them away. When the eggs **hatch**, 56 days later, she is nowhere near. The babies dig their way out of the sand at night and hurry down the beach to the sea. On the beach, predators such as crabs, dogs and vultures are waiting for them. In the **shallows**, sharks are lurking. Many baby turtles are caught. Very few survive to grow up into adults.

Baby hawksbill turtles are only 5 cm long. As soon as they hatch, they have to cross the beach and get out to sea as quickly as they can to avoid danger.

Battle for survival

On average, a green turtle lays 1800 eggs in its lifetime. Unfortunately, most of them never reach adulthood. 1400 eggs never hatch, 200 **hatchlings** die on the beach, 160 hatchlings die in the shallows and 37 hatchlings die in their first week at sea. Only 3 of the baby turtles will grow up to become adult turtles.

Caring crocs

Crocodiles are among the few reptiles that look after their babies for a while. A female Nile crocodile guards her nest until the eggs hatch. She does not eat at all during this time. After 90 days, the young crocodiles start squeaking inside their eggs. When the female hears this noise, she opens up the nest, picks up the babies in her mouth and gently carries them down to the water. Here she stays close by to protect them for the first six to eight weeks of their lives.

People once thought that female crocodiles ate their babies, because of the way they carry them in their mouths. They are, however, very gentle with them, and the babies are not harmed.

How do baby reptiles grow bigger?

Reptiles start life small. Inside the egg, the yolk gave them all the **nourishment** they needed. This helps them to survive for a short while after **hatching**, but soon they need to eat in order to grow bigger. Unlike mammals, reptiles cannot produce milk for their babies to suckle, so soon the babies have to start finding food for themselves.

What's on the menu?

All snakes are **carnivores**, or meat-eaters, that hunt other animals for food. Some, such as the king cobra, even eat other snakes. Many lizards are **omnivores**, eating a mixture of fruit and insects. Only tortoises are true **herbivores**: their heavy shells make them too slow to catch other animals, so they feed entirely on plants.

*Tortoises are plant eaters. They sometimes also gnaw on rocks that contain calcium. This important **mineral** helps their shells to grow and makes their eggshells stronger.*

Little Killers

Baby reptiles do not have to learn how to find food. Instead, they are born with all the skills they need. A baby rattlesnake knows how to kill its **prey** as soon as it is born. It has enough poison to kill a rat, though at this age it is too small to swallow rats. Instead it hunts smaller prey such as grasshoppers.

Just like an adult, a baby southern copperhead uses poison to kill its prey, before swallowing it.

A bigger bite

A baby alligator is about 25 cm long when it hatches. At this size it eats mostly insects and worms. When it reaches 1 metre long, it can catch frogs and small fish. At 2 metres long it can manage larger fish, water birds and rodents such as rats. At over 3 metres, a fully-grown alligator is big enough to catch a wild pig.

A change of food

As reptiles grow older, their choice of food changes. A baby green turtle starts life as a carnivore, eating fish and other small sea creatures. It grows up to become a vegetarian, eating mostly sea grass.

New skin for old

As a snake or lizard grows bigger, it sheds its old dry skin to reveal a shiny new one underneath. This is called **sloughing**. Sloughing first happens a few days after the reptile is born.

Most snakes shed their skins three or four times a year, and each time it takes two to three days. A snake's skin comes off in one long piece, but a lizard's peels away in ragged flakes and patches.

*When a snake, like this sand snake, sheds its skin, its eyes turn milky white. This is because a layer of fluid is trapped between the old eye **scale**, called a spectacle, and the new one. The snake cannot see until the old skin comes off.*

Shedding skin safely

A snake finds a safe, hidden spot to shed its skin. It starts by rubbing its head against a rock or hard object to loosen the scales around its mouth. It then crawls slowly forward so the rest of the old skin gradually rolls back and comes off inside out. Sea snakes rub against their own coils, so the old skin comes off in a twisted knot.

Baby's rattle

A rattlesnake's rattle is made of many loose pieces of old skin that make a rattling noise when the snake vibrates its tail. A baby rattlesnake is not born with a rattle. It has just one small button on the end of its tail. Each time it sheds its skin, another bit is added to the button. In this way the rattle becomes bigger as the snake grows older.

*A rattlesnake's rattle is made of old, dead skin. The noise it makes scares off **predators**.*

How do reptiles grow up in safety?

Most reptiles don't travel very far. Once a young reptile has found a safe, sheltered home, it may stay there for the rest of its life. Most reptiles make their home in a hidden place. Some snakes live in a hole in the ground. Many lizards prefer a crack in a rock or wall. Tortoises use a clump of grass or a low bush.

Dealing with danger

Life, even with a safe home, is still dangerous for young reptiles. Young reptiles that manage to escape from danger learn to be more careful in future. As they grow older, they become better at running, hiding or fighting. This helps them stay alive to grow up and live longer.

A wall makes a perfect home for baby wall lizards. They can shelter in the cracks, or bask on the warm stones. There is plenty of insect food nearby, too.

Fooling the enemy

If they are attacked, some young reptiles put on a show to fool their enemies and give them time to get away. A grass snake rolls over on its back and pretends to be dead, so that a **predator** loses interest. Some lizards even shed their tails when they are caught. The tail keeps wriggling to distract the attacker while the lizard runs away to safety. Most lizards can grow a new tail. This is known as regeneration.

When trapped by a predator, a frilled lizard spreads a frill of skin like an umbrella around its neck to look bigger. It also gapes its mouth wide to look fiercer.

When danger threatens, the armadillo girdled lizard retreats into a crack in a rock. If it is caught with nowhere to hide, it rolls itself into a spiky ball by gripping its tail between its teeth. It looks very difficult to swallow, so often a predator leaves it alone.

You can't see me

Some reptiles are so well **camouflaged** that they can hide right out in the open. The leaf-tailed gecko is coloured exactly like the bark of a tree. It rests against the trunk with its head pointing downwards, waiting to snap up its insect **prey**. Its flat tail and toes and the fringe of skin around its body are flattened against the bark, making it almost impossible to see. If a predator gets too close, the gecko scares it away by suddenly opening its mouth wide to show the bright orange lining.

Can you spot the lizard? The Madagascan leaf-tailed gecko is so well camouflaged it is difficult to see.

All at sea

The olive sea snake spends its life at sea, where it hunts small fish near the surface. It does not have a permanent home, and never comes to land. It sleeps, rests and gives birth to its babies underwater.

When is a reptile grown up?

A reptile is 'grown up' – or adult – when it is ready to start **breeding**, or having babies. This is called **maturity**. Different reptiles reach maturity at different speeds. Dwarf chameleons are ready to breed in nine months. For crocodiles it may take twelve to fifteen years.

Climate differences

The speed at which a reptile grows up depends upon the **climate** where it lives. Reptiles that live in cool climates grow fast during summer but stop growing during winter. In winter it is too cold for many reptiles to be outside, so they find a warm place to **hibernate**. This means that they take a long rest and don't eat anything or do any growing until spring.

*Red-eared terrapins hibernate in the mud at the bottom of ponds. Their body processes slow right down, so they do not need to breathe much. They get the little **oxygen** they need from the water through an opening under their bodies.*

Speeding up

Most snakes grow very fast at first. Rattlesnakes that are born in summer have to eat as much food as they can before the long winter hibernation. A timber rattlesnake can double its length in the first year of its life and reaches maturity after four years. Snakes that live in warm climates don't have to hibernate, so they grow all year round. A young python can grow three times its length during its first year of life.

Slowing down

As reptiles get older, they grow more slowly. They don't need so much energy, so they eat less often. A full-grown African rock python may eat fewer than ten times in a year. One big meal, such as an antelope, may take months to digest.

A full-grown water python can swallow a whole duck. By changing the position of its flexible (bendy) jawbones, it can open its mouth wide enough to swallow this enormous meal headfirst.

How do reptiles have babies?

Once reptiles are grown up, males and females get together to breed. First they must find each other. Some reptiles do this by smell. During the **breeding** season, the special time for **mating**, a female snake leaves a trail for the male to follow. He uses his tongue to pick up tiny particles of her scent from the air. A special **organ** in the roof of his mouth – called a Jacobson's organ – tells him they belong to a female. Other reptiles use colours: some male lizards display their bright patterns to females to show they are ready for breeding.

The male anole lizard, from Central America, perches on a tree trunk, puffs out his bright orange throat and nods his head up and down. This attracts the attention of a female. It also warns rival males to keep away.

Making a noise

Most reptiles are silent, but a few use noise in the breeding season to attract a mate. Male crocodiles thrash the water with their tails, spout jets of water out of their nostrils and raise their heads to bellow like bulls. Male barking geckos call from the entrances to their desert burrows. Their sharp clicking sound carries a long way in the still night air.

Although black mambas are highly venomous snakes, males never bite each other when they fight. Instead they have long wrestling matches.

Wrestling matches

Some male reptiles compete for females in a battle of strength. Females choose to mate with the winners, whose strength is then passed on to their babies. Male monitor lizards rear up on their hind legs and wrestle. Male tortoises push and bump each other, until sometimes one flips the other onto his back. Several male anacondas struggle with each other in one big wriggling ball, but only one of them will mate with the female and **fertilize** her eggs.

Mating dances

Before a male snake can mate with a female, he must get her interested. He moves his body over hers, rubbing his chin along her back and sides and flicking his tongue in and out. In some kinds of snake such as cobras, a male and female will rear up and sway together in a **courtship** dance. This goes on until the female gives a sign that she is ready. Then the male twines himself around her so mating can take place.

*Thousands of Canadian garter snakes **hibernate** together in underground dens to escape the cold. When they wake up in spring, they are ready for mating. For a few days, the ground is covered in wriggling snakes, as all the males struggle to mate with the females at the same time.*

Nesting

When reptiles have mated, the female must find a suitable place to lay her eggs. This is usually a warm, hidden spot, such as inside a hollow tree or under a rock. Some snakes return to use their favourite spot every year. A female king cobra makes a nest of her own. She scoops up a mound of rotting plants and digs two chambers inside. In the bottom one she lays her eggs, then she coils herself up in the top one. This keeps the eggs warm underneath her.

Helpful termites

Termites are insects that live in big mounds made of mud. A female water monitor lays her eggs inside a termite mound. The termites then repair the hole she has made. Inside, the eggs are protected, and stay at just the right warm temperature for **incubation**. At the start of the rainy season, the eggs **hatch** and the baby monitor lizards dig their way out.

It takes a female water monitor two to three days to lay up to 60 eggs inside a termite-mound nest.

23

Coming home

Sea turtles return to breed on the beaches where they were born. They travel long distances across the ocean, using currents to guide them. Courtship and mating take place in the **shallows**. Then, one moonless night when **predators** on the beach cannot see them, the females come ashore to lay their eggs. They dig a pit above the **high tide line**, beyond the waves, and lay their eggs. Finally, they cover them with sand and crawl back to the sea and swim away.

Hidden eggs

Like turtles, female tortoises bury their eggs. They dig a long pit in the ground, lay their eggs inside, cover them with soil and then use their bodies to pack the soil down. Soon there is no sign of the hidden eggs.

It takes two hours for a loggerhead turtle to lay her eggs, cover them and return to the sea. She will not come back for at least another three years.

How long do reptiles live?

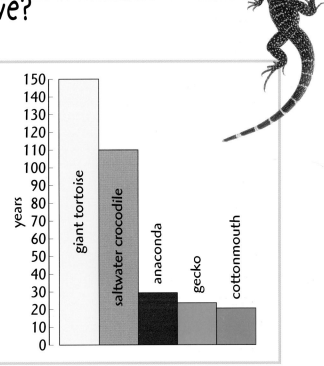

Many reptiles die young, when life is most dangerous for them. If they escape **predators** though, some can live for a very long time. Big reptiles live their lives very slowly. They don't use up much energy, so they can reach a ripe old age. Even little geckos can live for over 25 years, much longer than any mouse or bird of the same size. This graph shows how long different reptiles can live.

Old age giants

Reptiles never stop growing, and some reach an enormous size. Old leatherback turtles can weigh over 800 kg. The oldest saltwater crocodiles can reach over 6 metres long and weigh more than 1 tonne – as heavy as a black rhinoceros. Giant tortoises are the longest-living animals on Earth. Because they only eat plants, these slow-coaches use up very little energy to find their food. Their great size and thick shells protect them from predators.

The famous English scientist Charles Darwin saw giant tortoises when he visited the Gálapagos Islands in 1833. One tortoise that he brought back is still alive today, and living in Australia. Her name is Harriet, and she is over 170 years old!

People and reptiles

Most reptiles are perfectly harmless to people. Some are even useful to us. For example, snakes help to keep down the numbers of rats and mice that damage farmers' crops. Unfortunately, today the future of many reptiles is threatened. Some **species**, such as rare crocodiles, pythons and turtles are hunted for their skins. Many other species are threatened because people are destroying their **habitats** by cutting down forests or **polluting** the oceans. We should learn to understand reptiles, and protect them and their habitats. After all, reptiles have been on Earth for much longer than we have.

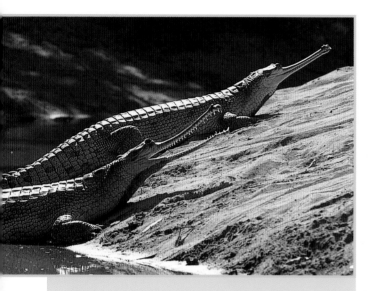

*The gavial is a rare relative of the crocodile that lives in Nepal. It has been hunted close to **extinction**.*

In the Mediterranean, noisy discos and bright hotel lights have scared away turtles from many of the beaches where they used to breed.

The cycle of life

No reptile lives for ever. Even so, by the time an adult reptile dies, it will have helped bring many more of its kind into the world. Over a lifetime, a female reptile, such as a turtle, may lay hundreds of eggs. Not all the eggs **hatch**, and many **hatchlings** die young, but those that survive – if they overcome all the dangers of life, such as predators and **pollution** – may eventually grow up to breed and lay eggs themselves. This is the cycle of life – from egg to adult – in which young are born, grow and produce young themselves. The cycle of life ensures the survival of each reptile species.

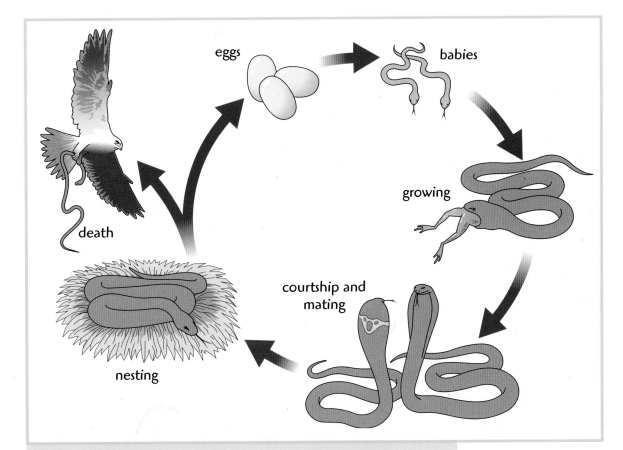

eggs

babies

growing

courtship and mating

nesting

death

All reptiles pass through the same stages in their life – from egg to adult.

Fact file

What is ...

• the biggest family?

Sea turtles lay the most eggs of any reptile. A leatherback turtle lays up to 1000 eggs in batches of 100–120 at eleven-day intervals. She then waits two to five years before **breeding** again.

• the biggest egg?

Pythons lay the biggest eggs of any reptile. They are round in shape, and about 10 cm in diameter – roughly the size of an orange.

• the most babies ever given birth to?

Some snakes can have a lot of live young. The record for any reptile is held by a puff adder from Kenya, which gave birth to 156 babies.

• the longest incubation?

The eggs of some lizards may **incubate** for over a year if development slows down during winter. Some chameleon eggs can take 377 days to hatch. In captivity, where the incubation temperature is kept exactly right all the time, they take about half this time.

• the biggest reptile?

It is hard to be sure how big reptiles can grow in the wild. The longest known snake is the reticulated python of south-east Asia, which occasionally reaches 9 metres, and big leatherback turtles can weigh over 900 kilos. The largest reptile all round is the saltwater crocodile, which may weigh over 1 tonne and measure 7 metres long.

Reptile classification

Classification is the way scientists group living things together. They divide all the reptiles in the world into four main groups.

- The biggest group of reptiles is the scaled reptiles, which includes snakes and lizards. There are over 6200 different **species**. They all have teeth, and shed their dry, scaly skin. Snakes, and some kinds of lizard, do not have legs.

- The second group is the shield reptiles, which includes tortoises, turtles and terrapins. There are 273 different species. They all have a hard protective shell, four legs and a horny beak instead of teeth.

- The third group of reptiles is the crocodiles and alligators. There are 23 different species. They all have tough skin covered in horny plates, long tails and four legs. Their long jaws have sharp teeth.

- There are only two species of tuatara in the fourth group. These lizard-like reptiles have four legs, a long tail and soft, scaly skin. Their skeleton shows that they have changed little in 200 million years.

The Komodo dragon of Indonesia is the world's biggest lizard. It measures up to 3 metres long, and weighs up to 160 kg – big enough to catch and eat a goat.

Glossary

amniotic fluid thick liquid inside an egg that protects the embryo

breeding having babies

camouflage colour or pattern that helps an animal blend in with its background

carnivore meat-eating animal

climate usual kind of weather in one place. For example, the Amazon rainforest has a warm, wet climate.

courtship special behaviour that takes place before mating

embryo very first stage of an animal's life, when it is still developing inside the egg

endoskeleton skeleton of bones inside an animal's body

extinct/extinction species of animal or plant has become extinct when there are none left on Earth

fertilization/fertilize when an egg is fertilized, an embryo begins to grow inside

habitat natural home of any living thing. A Nile crocodile's habitat is freshwater rivers.

hatch break out of an egg

hatchling baby animal when it has just hatched out of its egg

herbivore animal that eats just plants

hibernation/hibernate long period of winter rest for some animals, when it is very cold or there is not enough food

high tide line highest point that waves reach on a beach

incubation/incubate keeping an egg at the correct temperature for the baby inside to grow

mate when a male and female animal mate, the female's eggs join with a male sperm, and an embryo starts to grow

maturity being old enough to start breeding. Crocodiles reach maturity at about twelve years.

migration/migrate seasonal journey of animals from one place to another in order to find food or a good place for breeding

mineral chemical in the ground or in food, such as iron or calcium, that is important for growth

nourishment goodness and energy that comes from eating food

omnivore animal that eats plants and meat

organ part of the body that has a special job

oxygen gas in the air and dissolved in water, which living things need to breathe

pollution when something poisons or harms any part of the environment (world)

predator animal that hunts and eats other animals for food

prey animal that is hunted and eaten by a predator

regeneration/regenerate
    growing something again. The
    tail of a lizard is regenerated
    after it drops off.
scale tiny horny plate on the skin
    of a reptile or fish. A snake or
    lizard is covered with many scales
    packed together to form one
    tight, protective coat.
shallows area of shallow water,
    usually close to the shore

sloughing shedding an outer layer
    of skin from the body when it
    has become worn out
species type of animal that is
    able to breed with others of
    the same type
vertebrate animal with a
    backbone. Mammals, birds,
    reptiles, amphibians and fish are
    all vertebrates.

Find out more

Books

Eyewitness Guides: Reptile, Colin McCarthy (DK Publishing, 2000)
I Wonder Why Snakes Shed Their Skins, and other questions about
    reptiles, Amanda O'Neill (Kingfisher Books, 2000)
Reptiles, Anita Ganeri (Franklin Watts, 1994)
Eye Wonder: Reptiles, Barbara Taylor (DK Publishing, 2001)
Weird Wildlife: Reptiles, Jen Green (Belitha Press, 2002)

Websites

Worldwide Fund for Nature site:
 http://www.panda.org
Animal Planet site:
 http://www.animal.discovery.com/guides/animals/reptiles.html
Crocodilans, everything you wanted to know about crocodiles:
 www.crocodilian.com
A virtual zoo, with a great reptile house:
 http://www.library.thinkquest.org/11922/
The Education Planet search engine. Lots of links to reptile sites:
 www.educationplanet.com/search/Environment/Animals/Reptiles/

Index